THE CHRISTIAN AS CITIZEN

WORLD
CHRISTIAN
BOOKS

THE

CHRISTIAN

AS CITIZEN

by JOHN C. BENNETT

*Professor of Christian Theology and
Ethics, Dean of the Faculty, Union
Theological Seminary, New York*

ASSOCIATION PRESS, NEW YORK

ABOUT WORLD CHRISTIAN BOOKS

TODAY it is not enough to believe; it is necessary also to understand. From every part of the world comes the demand for books that will help the Christian to understand his faith, to find the answers to the questions that he and other men are asking, and to know how to present the faith to others. The series WORLD CHRISTIAN BOOKS is planned to help in this particular area of Christian need. The books are directed in the first place to the "younger churches," but the old distinction between younger and older churches no longer really holds. All churches are faced by the same problems. In all countries the same questions are being asked. The series is specially planned for those who are called to preach and teach, in the hope that the materials given in these books may help them to carry out their task more effectively. But the aim has also been to write so simply that ordinary members of the church who wish to study their faith may be able to use these books as individuals or in study groups and so to grow in knowledge and understanding.

The books are being published first in English, but it is intended that as soon as possible they should be made available in the main languages of the Christian world. Writers have been chosen from various countries and various branches of the church, with special emphasis on the younger churches. This means that there will be a variety of voices, but the aim and the hope is that through many minds and many tongues the faith of the church in its one Lord may be clearly set forth.

STEPHEN NEILL
General Editor

An American Preface

AMERICAN READERS of this book should realize that it was written originally for translation into the languages of the "younger churches" in Asia and Africa and the islands of the Pacific. Americans would, otherwise, be surprised at the emphasis in some of the illustrations. Several times the power of the "landlord" and the need of land reform are put ahead of the problems which preoccupy us. Also, I occasionally refer to America as though I were looking at it from outside. I refer to the need which other nations have of predicting the policy of both Russia and America. In Chapter 4, in dealing with the prospects of democracy, I have tried to put myself in the place of Christians who live in countries that have not inherited a strong democratic tradition or that have not been deeply influenced by Christianity. I am glad to leave the orientation of this book as it is in the American edition because I believe that one of our greatest needs today is to try to see the world as it appears to the nations which do not inhabit Europe or North America. I am no expert on these nations, but I can trace to a visit to many of them in 1950–51 some new habits of thinking about the issues discussed in this book.

Readers of my *Christian Ethics and Social Policy* will find especially in the first two chapters a similar structure of thought, but I hope that I have been able to push the discussion a few stages beyond the presentation in that book.

I am grateful to Bishop Stephen Neill, the General Editor of World Christian Books, for many helpful suggestions which will make the discussion more intelligible.

JOHN C. BENNETT

Contents

chapter **1**

The Christian's Social Responsibility

WHAT A CHRISTIAN can do as a citizen will differ from country to country, but the Christian's responsibility to take his citizenship seriously is everywhere the same. This responsibility is, basically, an extension of Christian love to those aspects of public life which affect for good or ill the welfare of one's neighbors. It can be seen also to be a response to the providential activity of God in the world; for God is the Lord of races and nations, of institutions and events, as well as of individual souls. God wills that his people should live under political institutions such as establish and preserve order; but, more than that, he wills that this order should be of the kind that is favorable to both social justice and spiritual freedom.

This Christian responsibility for society has been recognized throughout Christian history, but it has taken very different forms in different situations. It takes different forms in the Bible itself. In the period of the great prophets, especially while the Hebrew nation had some degree

11

of independence, the responsibility for justice in national life is greatly emphasized (e.g., Amos, Micah, Isaiah). In the New Testament there is little concern for social institutions or public policies. Concern for the *neighbor* who is a victim of such institutions or policies is clear in the Gospels. Also there is in the Gospels a radical reversal of our usual human attitudes toward wealth and privilege. The saying, "The last will be first, and the first last" (Matt. 20:16) applies to most of our conventional ways of arranging people. Jesus dealt with such institutions as the sabbath and the temple with a freedom which was in part the cause of his death. And yet the reform or reconstruction of social or political institutions is not a part of gospel teaching. In the Epistles there is emphasis on the obligation of the Christian to obey the political authorities. Both Paul and the author of the First Epistle of Peter stress this obligation. Neither had any thought of political action by Christian citizens to influence the structure of the empire or the policy of its rulers.

Two reasons made this role of passive obedience natural to Christians in the first century. The first is that they were a helpless minority, with no political power and with no opportunity to influence opinion among ruling groups in the empire. The other reason is that they fully expected this phase of human life, this age of history, to come to an early end with the establishment by God of his eternal kingdom. This expectation of a very short historical future made political issues, or the possibility of structural changes in society, appear relatively unimportant. To obey the authorities, except at those points where it was necessary to say, "We must obey God rather than men," and to endure patiently were sufficient for Christians who were waiting for an early end of history. The fact that the New Testament is almost wholly a nonpolitical book does create a problem for Christians who live in situations very differ-

12

ent from those which prevailed in the first century. If we understand why the New Testament is nonpolitical, we shall understand also the Christian responsibility to translate the essential social concern which is at the heart of it into terms that are relevant to the problems of the Christian citizen today.

Churches Behind the Times

In doing this, we shall be following the example of Christians in many periods and in many traditions. Ever since the Christian Church became an accepted part of the civilization of the Roman Empire (4th century A.D.), Christians have had to wrestle with the problems of Christian citizenship. Sometimes, indeed, they gave up the struggle, and chose to be monks or hermits, remote from the problems of the world; and yet most of those who made this choice continued to be part of a church which remained in the world, and many of them rendered their own contributions, direct or indirect, to the development of the culture and institutions of what was once called "Christendom."

The church during the period of its greatest power in Europe (11th–15th centuries) was mightily concerned about the social and political life of the world. It helped "to give form to life." Its ethic, partly influenced by ideas which had come not from the Bible but from the Greeks, was an uneasy compromise between the *agape,* love, of the New Testament, and the world of feudal powers, of society ordered in different levels of privilege, of private property, even of slavery. It partly tamed this world, but at the price of identifying Christianity and the church too closely with its culture, and of tolerating too much that was unjust in society. It did try to raise the world to a higher level, and it did develop an inclusive system of law for both personal and public life. It was a civilizing and conservative force

13

rather than a source of revolutionary criticism, though in its monastic movements at their best, something of the radical Christian criticism of society was kept alive.

The great Reformers (16th century) did not, in intention, break with the medieval church's sense of responsibility for society as a whole. But the Reformation came at a time when profound changes were taking place in the whole of culture. The division between Protestant and Roman Catholic in the church was one factor, but only one, in these changes. We must remember that this was the period when the geographical discoveries greatly enlarged the world known to the church; when modern nations with their ideas of sovereignty were being born; when the revival of secular learning undercut the central place of Christian faith in the mind of Europe; when the beginnings of science and technology and of modern capitalism already foreshadowed the development of vast new forces which have since remade the external life of the Western world. Many of these changes did, on balance, make for a better life for men. But the churches in their thought did not keep up with them, and so were in the main unable to guide or restrain them.

This was not wholly true of countries in which Christian faith continued to influence the culture and the moral assumptions of the people and their political institutions. But even in those countries there was a long period in which economic life was, as R. H. Tawney says, a "lost province" of the church.

New Christian Attitudes

There has been a profound change in the past century in the church's own understanding of its responsibility for the institutions of society. This change came especially in relation to economic life. The new attitude appeared most clearly in the late nineteenth century in Europe and America, in both Protestantism and Roman Catholicism. It was associated with many voluntary Christian movements for social reform and economic justice. Pope Leo XIII (1878–1903) was the great Roman Catholic leader whose encyclicals on social and economic problems mark the beginning of a new era in the life of that Church, especially in industrialized countries. In the United States the Social Gospel was the name given to the Protestant form of this same interest. This social concern of the churches has been given sanction and new organs of expression in the ecumenical movements. The great conferences at Stockholm (1925), Jerusalem (1928), Oxford (1937), Madras (1938), Amsterdam (1948), Evanston (1954), have proved to be remarkable sounding boards for this social concern, and they have developed a considerable body of Christian social teaching with wide support.

The events of the past twenty-five years have forced Christians, in many traditions to which this social concern was most alien, to take it seriously. Bitter experience under the National Socialist tyranny in Germany (1933–45) taught many Christians for the first time that they could not be indifferent to the problems of political structure. The rise of Communism has forced upon many other Christians the realization that they have been far too slow in facing the problems of economic justice. The most recent development has been the rather sudden and too-long-delayed awakening of the churches to the shame and injustice of racial and color discrimination and segregation.

That which on the whole distinguishes the most recent Christian thinking from the attitudes of the great churches in the past is the conviction that Christian responsibility for society includes a responsibility for radical criticism of the existing order. This has led to organized efforts— usually taking political forms—to change the structures of society so that they may be more favorable to justice and to fraternal relations among men. Christians in some traditions were so much influenced by the prevailing optimism regarding the possibilities of social progress that they came to expect too much, and often they were far too unaware that evil as well as good might spring from programs for social change. But it was right for them to look to the future with hope, rather than to accept as unalterable the age-old structures, under which benefits and privileges had been confined to a small segment of the human race.

Three factors at least have influenced the church from outside, and have forced a re-examination of older Christian ideas about society.

One was the fact that society itself was changing rapidly. The old static institutions have either disappeared or have been modified beyond recognition. The development of democratic political institutions, the growing power of the organized industrial workers, the pressure of the national aspirations of the people of Asia and Africa, have changed the face of the world. The mere fact of large-scale change has swept away some old-fashioned interpretations of divine providence. No longer can it be assumed that the existing order, because it is here, is divinely appointed. Ideas of the divine right of kings, of the divine right of the holders of property, of the divine right of the imperial powers, of the divine right of the white race, are no longer plausible even to those who have profited from them. The old rhyme, "God bless the squire and his relations; And help us all to keep our stations," did express a situation which once existed in England. Today such a jingle would meet with nothing but ridicule. In the United States in 1860 there were sober theologians in the southern states who defended slavery on biblical and theological grounds. In the same year there were sober theologians in

16

the northern states who taught that the so-called laws of *laissez faire* capitalism were laws of God, and that it was wrong for men to tamper with wage scales which were dictated by the free market. Today in most of the world the climate has so changed that such ideas as these are dead. Christians have been forced to think different thoughts; and in doing so they have often found that their new thoughts are more consistent with essential elements in their faith than were the more traditional ideas of society.

A second factor is that the people who have been neglected and exploited in the past have not only gained power to press for many of the changes to which I have referred, but they have also acquired a voice so that they could say how the world appeared to them. They have been able to talk back to those who had kept to themselves the privilege and the power. They have been able to speak to the conscience of the church and to win much support for their aspirations. They have been able to show how hollow many of the expressions of Christian love were when they took a paternalistic form, and raised no question concerning the power of those at the top, which enabled them to do good things for others. The results of paternalism have not all been bad, and it has often been wise to distribute power gradually; but when paternalism is a sop to the consciences of those whose chief desire is to maintain their power, it is the source of moral confusion. Today paternalism—whether it is constructive or merely a cloak for superior power and privilege—is on the defensive everywhere in the world. Christians have been forced to rethink the meaning of Christian love in the context of power and privilege.

The third factor was the clearer recognition of the effect of external conditions on the development of persons. It is not possible to separate soul from body or the whole person from the environment. Christians cannot, indeed, admit that man's nature is entirely determined by the environment in which he lives. They know that the mature soul can transcend cramping and destructive circumstances, that neither persecution nor sword need destroy the spirit. They know that men often are at their best, that men may become heroes and saints, when external conditions are at their worst. Also, it is possible for the church or for more informal Christian communities to create an immediate environment within the larger environment of society as a whole, and so to enable Christians to grow in grace and to become strong in spirit even when the world is externally most unfavorable to the Christian life. Yet, after we have said these things, it is important to remember that political and social conditions can be such as to cut the church off from all but the inner core of faithful Christians, and to cripple its work among its own youth. Even the Christian family is no sure oasis, which can protect children and young people against the influence and teaching of a state hostile to the Christian faith. The totalitarian state can reach very early into the family and turn children against the faith and traditions of their parents. The Christian must be concerned about the nature of the state, partly because he knows what some kinds of tyranny can do to the development of children and to family life.

Also, intelligent love for the neighbor must be concerned about the effect of economic institutions and policies upon persons. Here, again, the effect of poverty and malnutrition and slum conditions on children presents the most obvious challenge. But our interest should be much broader. When it becomes apparent that any persons are hungry or thirsty or strangers or naked or sick or in prison as a result of conditions which can be brought to an end by changing economic institutions or by corporate action of any kind, the Christian must translate the injunctions of the gospel into such action. This is itself a natural consequence of Christian commitment, wherever such action is possible.

There was a period in modern industrialized countries when some Christians assumed that if people were unemployed or in economic distress, it was their own fault, and that the most suitable thing to do was to exhort them about it. Today we know that persons are often the victims of large-scale forces which they cannot control, that unemployment often comes upon them as a kind of external fate. Archbishop William Temple (1882–1944) saw these things more clearly than most modern churchmen. He was haunted by the effect of long continued unemployment upon people. He was not so much distressed by the poverty which unemployment brought (since this could be dealt with by social services), as by its effect upon the spirits of men, causing them to believe that they were no longer wanted. "This," Temple said, "is the thing that has power to corrupt the soul of any man not already far advanced in saintliness." He explained this by saying: "Because the man has no opportunity of service, he is turned in upon himself and becomes, according to his temperament, a contented loafer or an embittered self-seeker." [1]

One could go on at length to show the ways in which environment or the climate of a culture can tempt or weaken or corrupt the human spirit. It is important for the spirit to be strengthened to meet these threats. But churches and Christians, who can influence the form of the environment and the climate of the culture, have a responsibility also to do what they can to change or neutralize those factors in the life of society which have power to hurt or corrupt. There is no reason to fear that they will be so successful that they will remove all the hardships and temptations which, within limits, may be the means

---

[1] *Christianity and Social Order* (Penguin), p. 12.

19

of discipline. There will remain enough of these and to spare!

The Biblical Imperatives

I have suggested some reasons for believing that Christian citizenship in our time must involve more than the acceptance of conventional duties *within the social order as it is*. It must involve an active concern for social justice and for the freedom of persons. It must involve, where this is possible, organized action, often political action, to guide or to transform the institutions and structures of society.

I do not want to overemphasize the novelty of this concern for the radical transformation of social structures. But, so far as the great churches are concerned, it is in emphasis new. It represents the translation of essential biblical convictions and commands into terms appropriate to situations in which Christians do not expect the world to end tomorrow, in which changes are possible, and in which churches and Christians have influence in varying degrees on public opinion, on social structures, and on political policies.

The essential biblical convictions and commands which are the basis of Christian citizenship can be summarized as follows:

1. The faith that God, as known to us in Christ, is the Lord of human history, of nations, and of events; and that his purpose includes righteousness in the corporate as well as in the personal relations of men.

2. The commandment of love, which involves sensitive caring for the welfare and dignity of all men as neighbors, and service to them both in direct personal relationships and in efforts to improve the external conditions which affect their lives.

3. The call to repentance—repentance for all, since we are all in a measure involved in the corporate sin of our nations and civilizations; repentance which is a

call to transform what can be transformed for the sake of the neighbor.

4. The Christian understanding of sin, which includes the recognition that all men are inclined to give more weight than they should to the interests of their own social group, and to deceive themselves, while they take advantage of others who have less power than themselves. It is this tendency that makes it essential to support the difficult processes by which power is distributed, and by which as large a part of the population as possible is given a share in making the decisions by which its life is governed.

5. The recognition that the neighbor whom we serve is no disembodied spirit, but a whole person who lives as a member of a community. His soul is affected by what happens to his body, and the very substance of his personality is drawn in large part from his social relations.

chapter 2

From Christian Faith to Political Decisions

THIS CHAPTER will deal with the relationship between Christian faith and ethics on the one hand, and on the other with the decisions which Christians must make as citizens in public life. This relationship is by no means easy to chart, because Christian love seems to belong to a world that is remote from the pride and self-interest and the power struggles of the political order. The political and economic life of nations may seem at best to be governed by rules so different from the gospel that Christians who seek to be true to the gospel teaching about love will find it best to try to live apart from it. But this is impossible, and to attempt it is one of the surest ways of sinning against love.

The clash between Christian principles and the rules that seem to govern the public life of our nations and communities is only a part of the problem. There is also the fact that there are many aspects of our life for which there is no sure Christian guidance, no direct guidance from the Bible or from the great theological traditions.

22

Nearly every important decision in public or national life has technical aspects, concerning which the Christian as Christian or the church as church has no special wisdom. To act wisely, it is necessary to have either expert knowledge of the actual situation, or the kind of awareness which comes to those who have had first-hand experience of that situation. The Christian may be more sensitive to human aspects of the situation than the expert, and he may be helped by his faith to ask deeper questions than the expert is likely to ask. But this sensitivity and this questioning cannot take the place of expert knowledge and specific experience. The technical aspect of these decisions also involves understanding of the probable consequences of the decision, once it has been taken. There is a body of expert knowledge concerning what in common language is called "cause and effect." The Christian may know that something should be done to prevent unemployment or to check a rapid fall in the purchasing power of money, or to discover the best ways of making agriculture more productive; but there is nothing in Christian faith and ethics to provide him with the technical knowledge on which alone a right answer can be based. If the experts agree, a solution may easily be found; but it often happens that the experts give contradictory advice. The more controversial the question, the more the experts themselves are likely to confuse the strictly technical issues with the dominant presuppositions and interests of the nations or classes which have formed their outlook on life.

More difficult than the technical issues in the narrow sense are the many questions which can be settled neither by expert opinion nor by a clear Christian moral judgment. I have in mind the problem of foreseeing what human behavior is likely to result from the adoption of a particular policy. The policies of many nations at present are based upon calculations concerning the nature of Communism; concerning the real intentions of Russia or China or America; concerning the effect of military preparations or the lack of them upon the prospects for peace; concerning the possibility of a democratic process by which the standard of living of certain countries can be raised; concerning the effect of particular economic structures upon incentives to work and to produce; concerning ways of overcoming political corruption; concerning the effect of various cultural changes on the growth of population. There is no unmistakably *Christian* answer to any of the questions which these issues raise, and yet our decisions as citizens depend upon our calculations as to what the answers are—and many of them are extremely fateful decisions.

The difference between the technical issues and the broader questions to which Christian faith provides no direct answers can be illustrated by referring to one problem: the problem of raising the standard of living of a particular area. There are here strictly technical questions touching the natural resources of the area, the effect of proposed agricultural methods on production in that area, and the extent of the capital investment that will be required. The experts can give some estimate of the improvements that can be expected, given reasonable co-operation by the people in the area, if various methods are used and a certain amount of capital is made available. But there are many questions which are more complicated or dependent on factors that are very difficult to define, and yet in relation to which those responsible for policy must calculate as accurately as possible. What are the best methods of securing co-operation from the people in that area? What will be the effect of a rise in the standard of living on the culture of the people concerned? How can capital be invested in the situation, without creating relations of dependence on another nation which will suggest something of the old and much hated imperialism? How can those who supply capital from within the country be prevented from taking far more than their due share of the profits? What will be the effect of a rising standard of living on the growth of population? What will be its effect upon the attractiveness of Communism to the people in the area? There is no sure Christian answer to any one of those questions.

It is obvious that if there are so many questions for which there are no distinctively Christian answers, there will be differences of judgment among Christians. These differences will come in part from the direction of attention to different factors in the situation, in part from differences of calculation. We must accept the fact that such differences will arise, even when people are as objective and honest as it is possible for the human mind to be.

We must also allow for other sources of the differences; and we must recognize that, in the case of any individual or of any group of Christians who are like-minded, there is a great mixture of all the sources of difference to which I refer here. There are deep preferences among Christians, as among others, for one emphasis as opposed to another in matters of social policy—preferences for order and security over against freedom and flexibility; preferences for the traditional and the tested over against new experiments; preferences for the evils of which we have had experience to those which are unknown but feared. There are also preferences which have their roots in national or class interest, or in the narrow interests of one's own family or immediate group. Those who are victims of injustice or oppression under one order of society are likely to assume that any change will be for the better; and to those who have been more favored by society, they may seem reckless in their demands for change. Those whose interests are threatened by some proposed change in the social order can easily use the technical arguments against it as a smoke screen to cover up the self-interest that is the real ground of their objection to the change. Wherever there are two sides to a question, the line which we all most naturally follow is to emphasize the side that is most in harmony with our own interests, or with the interests of the groups whose influence has formed our minds. This can easily happen without conscious dishonesty.

Enough has been said to show that this problem of relating Christianity to our decisions as citizens, to our votes, to our various political loyalties, is not easy and the solution is not obvious. This problem lies behind the extremely mixed pattern we find in Christian history, in the course of which Christians and churches have found a great variety of solutions. There is no one inevitable Christian solution —this is part of the problem. The three most dangerous and misleading ways of dealing with the problem are, first, to deny its existence; secondly, to assume that the answers which happen to come to our minds or which make most sense in our culture are *the* Christian answers; and thirdly, to assume that, because of all of this confusion, the Christian has no responsibility to find any answers.

Toward Christian Citizenship

I shall now suggest a way of mapping out the positive relation between Christian faith and ethics on the one hand and our life as citizens on the other.

There are three factors on the deepest level, which I shall call Perspective, Motive, and Corrective. These affect our basic purpose and outlook. Several steps will then be suggested by which we may move from these to concrete action in society.

Perspective

Christians must live, decide, and act in a world which they know to be God's world. They stand always under God's judgment, and they live in hope. They understand

26

that God transcends every culture, every power, every social group, every ideal, every church. "Behold, the nations are like a drop from a bucket, and are accounted as the dust on the scales" (Isa. 40:15). Always we stand before the warning against idolatry. The first commandment, "Thou shalt have no other gods before me," is the place where our understanding of Christian citizenship must begin. It is in our preference for our own culture, our own nation, our own social system, as against others that idolatry of the more subtle kind often appears.

Our first step as we try to discover a Christian orientation to public life is to lay ourselves open to God's judgment, which is above every interest and every ideal that is dear to us. This openness to God's majesty and to God's transcendent judgment can be the beginning of political wisdom, though we cannot deduce from it any particular conviction about what we should do tomorrow. We can be protected by it against many narrow convictions, which are based upon the tendency to make idols out of the things that are most familiar to us or are in harmony with our own interests. Much one-sidedness in social idealism partakes of this kind of idolatry. The Christian can easily see this in the case of the Communist, who does make a god out of his own ideological and social scheme. But any Christian may find himself in some degree making a god of political independence, of economic free-enterprise, of national security, of some particular governmental system, of the claims of his own nation.

The Christian perspective includes hope that is based upon God's act of redemption in Christ. Of itself, this provides no social solutions; but it does make it possible for Christians to continue to act in hope as Christian citizens, whatever the external circumstances, because it is not only upon political success or political failure that everything depends. Sometimes in the current discussion of the Chris-

27

tian hope, there has been an effort to extract from Christian hope more direct guidance on social problems than it can yield. It does not offer guidance so much as it offers a basis for morale in the broadest sense of the word. If we believe that everything depends upon our success or failure in this or that social effort, we are likely to become so anxious that we cannot do our best work. At times we are likely to despair. The ultimate faith that God has redeemed and will redeem, that the future is in his hands, that neither totalitarianism nor nuclear war can separate us from the love of God in Christ Jesus, is the only antidote to the distortions which anxiety or despair introduces into our life, and into our judgments about what we should do.

The Christian perspective includes not only hope for the future but awareness of God's forgiveness now. One of the most common errors that Christians make is the assumption that their integrity, and what the theologians have called their "justification," depend upon their finding the wholly good social cause to serve, or the social decision which is so evidently right that no doubt as to its rightness can be raised. Christians should be well warned, by their own understanding of the universality and persistence of sin in human life, that no such cause and no such decision exist. Yet I believe that, for many modern Protestants, the religious equivalent of Martin Luther's quest for perfect righteousness through monastic discipline is precisely this quest for such a cause or such a decision. One of the ways in which today we can see the meaning of "justification by faith" is that it enables us to live amidst the inescapable evils of our common life, choosing programs and identifying ourselves with groups which in part embody these evils, and yet to do so with the knowledge that, if our hearts are open to his love, God will accept us as we are. He does not wait, before accepting us, until the perfect cause or the perfectly right decision has been found. And it is quite clear that to refuse to identify ourselves with any cause, or to refuse to make any decision, is not to obey the Lord of history, who asks us to do what finite and sinful creatures can do to serve their neighbors in love.

Motives and Intentions

The motives and intentions of Christians, in public life as in private life, should be controlled by commitment to God's purpose of love for all persons. Wholeness of commitment is difficult both in private life and in public life. In both private and public life our love for our neighbors is easily displaced or distorted by pride and self-interest and by many forms of hostility. In public life there are available more elaborate rationalizations of pride and self-interest and hostility; but I doubt if it is much more difficult for our motives and intentions to be governed by love in the one case than in the other. Experts in the treatment of mental and emotional sickness have shown us how deep the problem of hostility, hidden or disguised, often is in the most intimate personal relations. Openness to the grace of God and gratitude for his love for us are the springs of Christian motive; and the healing that comes from our appropriation of the Christian understanding of justification by faith is as important for us in relation to the ambiguities of our motives and intentions as it is in relation to the ambiguities of our policies and decisions in the social order.

There has been in recent years much discussion concerning the nature of Christian love. For the purposes of this study, Christian love clearly involves caring for the welfare and dignity of all who are affected by what we do or leave undone. There is no limit to the range of this caring. It should extend to those whom we meet face to face, and to vast multitudes whom we may never see. It should extend to those who share our background and interests and whom we readily understand, and to those whose background is entirely different and whose interests are opposed to ours. It should extend to friends and to enemies.

The problems of adjustment of the claims of those for whom we have a special responsibility and the claims of those who are at a distance are in practice very puzzling. The problem of how we should deal with enemies and opponents, when there is between them and us a conflict in which, as we see it, freedom or justice for whole nations is at stake, is always difficult. And yet, even in the hardest cases of this sort, there is no place for hate; and when divided by conflict from any human beings, we should never forget that they are human, that they stand with us before God who loves both them and us. The reality of Christian love even in dark times of conflict may be tested, when chance encounters between individuals who are opponents or enemies take place, or when the opportunities for reconciliation appear after the external conflict has come to an end. Christians never can write off another human being for political reasons, however much they may be opposed to him, and however much they must seek to avoid being used by him for his political ends. I believe that this is one of the great differences between Christianity and Communism. There is for the Communist no dimension in which the opponent still remains an object of respect and love.

In public life, Christian love has to be related to the existing situation by means of general human values or principles, the recognition of which is much broader than is the acceptance of the claims of Christian love. I refer to such values as peace or order, justice, freedom, and what may be called the material conditions of human welfare. Theologians debate endlessly as to the manner in which knowledge about these values comes to us, and as to the relation between them and love. All theologians make use of them, whatever their views as to their source and origin. One thing is clear: Christians have no monopoly of these values, though in the context of Christian faith each may take on

30

on advanced levels of culture, in the life of reason, in man's idealism, and not least in the life of religion.

Love should be the chief motive in the Christian life, but humility should be the chief corrective. It may seem that the emphasis here on self-criticism, repentance, and humility is in danger of paralyzing us. If this does happen, it means that this emphasis has been taken out of the total context of Christian faith. Obedience and love, hope and forgiveness, should be sufficient to overcome any such paralysis. Also, we can say that humility may often represent something positive. It may make the most needed contribution to the situation. It may create openness to change. It may create the possibility of negotiation to break a stalemate. It may develop an atmosphere in which the most creative steps become possible. There is no greater obstacle to justice than self-righteous hardness, which protects the conscience of the strong against the claims of the weak and exploited. There is no more destructive nationalism than the nationalism that is mixed with the hardness of spiritual pride. There is no greater ruthlessness than the ruthlessness of those who are absolutely sure that they alone are right, and who sincerely believe that since they alone have the key to justice and peace, it is their duty to impose their will on others.

It is one of the most destructive aspects of Communism that the Communists sincerely believe that they have the only clue to history and the only program for human betterment, that all opponents are mere obstacles to be rendered powerless or removed, and that if they can only succeed in pushing through their program, their very ruthlessness in doing so will cause the dictatorship of the proletariat and all its instruments of ruthlessness to wither away. One of the deepest differences between Christianity and Communism is that Communists have in their system no basis for seeing that repentance may be demanded of them, even while they are serving the revolution; and no way of seeing themselves and their opponents as standing alike under the judgment of God, since both alike share in the sin which is common to all men. The most terrible corruption of Christianity comes about when Christians forget this aspect of their faith, and concentrate only upon the sin of heretics, unbelievers, enemies, or opponents.

Power—Its Uses and Dangers

In the first chapter attention was called to the need of recognizing how far power can distort human relations. Power as such is neither wholly good nor wholly bad, and it is necessary that there be power in both economic and political life. But power must be subject to criticism, and there must be some means by which it can be checked. No one has put more effectively the point that needs to be made here than Abraham Lincoln, who said: "No man is good enough to govern another without that other's consent." He was speaking of slavery, but his words apply to any social structure which enables one person or group to exercise arbitrary power over other persons or groups. Lincoln was a better theologian in this context than most orthodox theologians of his time.

There are temporary relations between people which, because of differences of age and experience, involve the use of power without the consent of those over whom it is exercised; but even in these cases it must not be arbitrary. In the most obvious case, that of the relationship between parents and young children, the community should take responsibility to protect the children against cruel abuses of such power. The power of landlords over tenants, and of employers over employees, should always be criticized and checked by those over whom it is exercised. Tenants need to be protected by law against arbitrary evictions, and employees need to be protected both by law and by

34

the strength of trade unions. Christian landlords and Christian employers should be the first to recognize the need for protection of those over whom they have power; for, no matter how good their intentions, they are seldom able to put themselves in the place of their tenants or their employees. It cannot be said that Christian landlords and employers have usually advocated this kind of restraint on themselves. It is a part of the sinful blindness of most of us that we do not readily understand such needs in advance; but at least we should recognize them in time to accept the social changes, which others demand as necessary to protect them against our own blindness, self-centeredness, and inertia.

The Christian Church can help Christians to overcome some of those distortions of their minds which are caused by narrow interests, by nationalism, or by ignorance of cultures other than their own. This is one of the great contributions of the World Council of Churches, which helps Christians from different nations and cultures to take each other seriously, so that each may see the world as it appears to the other. Within single nations this can happen also where a church includes those who represent different social groups or classes. In many situations local churches are made up of only one social group, and thus they tend to harden the narrow outlook of their members. This is one reason why the local church needs to be made aware of itself as sharing in the life of the larger, ecumenical Christian community.

Toward Concrete Decision

So far I have discussed those contributions of Christian faith and ethics to our life as citizens which form our minds and hearts, and which should always form the background for our concrete decisions. The church can work most easily in this area of motives and intentions, of basic prin-

35

ciples and attitudes. But this is not enough for the church as church, and it is even less adequate for the Christian who is called upon to decide, to vote, to act on the most perplexing practical issues. Our discussion must be carried three steps further:

1. *Christian criticism of the existing situation* should be both rigorous and concrete. This is an essential part of the prophetic function of the church. Criticism need not be wholly negative, nor should it be expressed in a scolding and self-righteous spirit. The churches themselves are involved in the very evils which they criticize in the social order. Precision in calling attention to the actual injustices and corruptions to be found in the community, and to the more subtle evils or temptations which characterize the culture, is the surest way of preventing general principles from becoming harmless platitudes. The report of the Oxford Conference on Church, Community, and State (1937) in discussing this matter of negative criticism on the part of the church said: "Here it is important not to impute motives or to denounce individuals (except where special circumstances call for such denunciation) but to present facts in such a way that they speak for themselves to the individual conscience" (p. 102). The church should be an expert on the human effects of any institution or policy. It should know what this or that institution and policy does to the character of persons, to the well-being of families.

It may often seem disturbing that it is easier to show what is wrong than to prescribe a program for putting it right. Obviously, one can discover what are the effects on human lives of existing institutions and policies, even though it may be very difficult to predict what the effects of alternative institutions and policies might be. But this apparently negative attitude should not cause the Christian too grave concern, since, to quote the Oxford report again, "what in isolation seems to be purely destructive criticism is a necessary part of the total process by which constructive change is brought about" (p. 102). In any situation there is needed an advocate for the people who are most wronged, and a critic of the moral and spiritual influences of the culture. The churches should fill both of these roles; they should stimulate their members to find new ways of doing things, and solutions for the problems to which they call attention. Churches as churches do not possess the technical knowledge, without which it is impossible to prescribe the changes in detail; but they can stir the conscience of the community, beginning with the consciences of their own members, to take positive action.

There is always a danger that Christian realism about human nature and about the social order will cause Christians to develop, perhaps without intending to do so, a double standard for private and public life; one standard for the state and another for the family or for personal relations. It is quite true that we cannot expect the state to be controlled by *agape,* Christian love, though it is not impossible for the *agape* of many of its citizens to influence its policy for the better, as for example when the state decides that it will do what it can to provide for the children of all classes equal access to education and to the means of health. But, even though there will always be a great distance between Christian love and the policies of states and the behavior of all power groups, those policies and that behavior should be kept under the criticism of love.

Even though the immediate standard by which they must be judged is justice rather than love, every system of justice needs constantly to be criticized in the light of the claims of love. Justice quickly becomes too static, unable to meet the changing needs of people, because by its very nature it must deal with people impersonally according to some established principle. Even when justice is identified with the cause of the oppressed, it often loses sight of human beings as persons, both among the oppressed and among the oppressors. In the recent writings of the great Swiss theologian, Karl Barth, there has been a strong tendency to stress *man,* the human being as such, against principles and programs and causes, a tendency which should be welcomed everywhere in the church. He writes:

> Since God Himself became man, man is the measure of all things, and man can and must only be used and, in certain circumstances, sacrificed for man. Even the most wretched man—not man's egoism but man's humanity—must be resolutely defended against the autocracy of every mere "cause." Man has not to serve causes: causes have to serve man.[2]

2. The next step, as we move closer to practical decisions, is for churches to emphasize *proximate goals, immediate objectives,* which are implied in Christian faith and love in relation to the actual situation in which the churches live. These goals are similar to what the ecumenical literature of recent years has called "middle axioms." Dr. J. H. Oldham was the first to give currency to that phrase in this context. He meant by a "middle axiom" something that is more definite than a universal ethical principle, and less specific than a program that includes legislation and political strategy. He says of middle axioms:

> They are an attempt to define the directions in which, in a particular state of society, Christian faith must express itself. They are not binding for all time, but are provisional definitions of the type of behavior required of Christians at a given period and in given circumstances.[3]

The best way in which to make this concept of the middle axiom or proximate goal clearer is to give some examples.

---

[2] *Against the Stream,* p. 35.
[3] *The Church and Its Function in Society,* p. 210.

These goals may be relevant to a particular region rather than to the whole world.

In many regions today, the most urgent problems are connected with systems of land ownership and tenure. In 1952 there was held in Lucknow, India, a very representative Christian conference which dealt with some of the social problems in East Asia. This conference expressed agreement on the following objectives in regard to land tenure:

1. Abolition of the old feudal landlord system is necessary. There is in most cases no moral justification for compensation of the landlord by the state or the cultivator. Justice for the peasant requires that he should not be burdened with new indebtedness due to compensation. [A note is added here which says that "this does not mean a general endorsement of expropriation of property but relates solely to the specific situation here encountered."]
2. Ownership by cultivators of farms in appropriate subsistence size is the goal.
3. Freedom from the money lender through making credit available to the peasant on cheap terms.
4. Utilization without delay of unutilized land.
5. Provision of land for landless peasants and settlement of homeless.

These problems have not been much discussed in the church on a world scale, but this agreement by Christians in the areas where land reform is a matter of highest priority is notable. The Evanston report (1954) on "Social Problems" endorsed these goals. What was said at Lucknow about refusal of compensation to landlords whose lands have been taken away can hardly be raised to a universal principle of justice, as indeed the note attached to it admits. Is it not possible that, in situations where vast private estates are involved, compensation should have in view the needs of the owners as human beings rather than the full value of their holdings? Some compensation within the limits suggested might, in many cases, be demanded by justice, and it could well prevent the community from being torn apart by class hatred.

RACIAL SEGREGATION

An example of a middle axiom or "proximate goal" on which almost all the readers of this book are likely to agree is the disappearance of all legal barriers by which, in a single country, citizens of different racial origin are kept in separation from one another without their own consent. In several countries it is the most burning question of practical politics. Yet the acceptance of the goal does not suggest the precise methods by which such segregation is to be overcome. In the United States the Supreme Court has affirmed the goal of racial integration so far as publicly supported schools are concerned. Under the circumstances, involuntary segregation cannot be overcome without establishing inclusive, interracial schools. This means that the government will have to enforce racial integration in schools on many people who strongly oppose the principle involved. So, the practical question arises as to how fast the law should move in enforcing integration. In such a context, when does law become self-defeating? Should a time schedule be arranged for the enforcement of integration in relation to the proportion of the races in the population of a given area? We may ask similar questions in any part of the world where Christians recognize the obligation to overcome racial segregation. Here is a clear objective, but Christians may naturally differ in their answers to those questions. The important thing is that they should not ask the questions merely to cause delay, merely to obstruct the attainment of the goal.

40

In industrialized countries the most urgent problem is the preservation of sufficient economic stability to prevent large-scale unemployment. It has become very widely recognized that it is the responsibility of the national community, working through its government, as far as possible to prevent unemployment. Christians as Christians have no special knowledge as to how this can best be done, but they can regard this objective as one for which they should work.

SELF-GOVERNMENT

The development toward self-government on the part of the peoples who are now under foreign rule is another objective of this kind. There is no principle known to Christians on the basis of which it is possible to determine exactly how rapidly this development should take place; but they do know that it is easy to find excuses for postponement, and that, therefore, it is usually desirable for those who hold the power to commit themselves to a definite timetable. There is no general rule concerning the best units of self-government. In other words, the principle of self-government need not mean the breaking up of a large territory into small independent units, as was done when the principle of "self-determination" was applied to eastern Europe after World War I. Also, the relation between self-government and regional or world-wide federations should remain an open question, and not be settled for all time in terms of absolute national sovereignty.

These are a few examples of "middle axioms" or "proximate objectives." These are objectives concerning which the Christian mind has in some measure become clarified in large segments of the church. No formulation of these

41

objectives should be allowed to harden, or to be regarded as a kind of Christian law.

We may be able to see what is meant by this defining of goals for Christians and churches, if we notice that the process of defining them consists in large part of reducing the number of the alternatives which are open to us as Christians. The Amsterdam Assembly (1948), in its well-known criticism of both Communism and *laissez faire* capitalism, condemned both a consistent economic collectivism and a consistent economic individualism; and pointed toward a broad path for experiment which, while the emphasis may differ from country to country, would be a mixed economy rather than a rigidly fixed economic system such as Communism, Socialism, or Capitalism. The Evanston Assembly (1954) avoided Amsterdam's reference to Communism and Capitalism as the two antagonistic systems, but its report pointed in the same direction.

In another area of problems we may say that Christians should be committed at the same time to the prevention of a third world war and to the limiting as far as possible of the power of totalitarianism in the world. Each of these objectives has great influence on the other. There is involved here a narrowing of alternatives; since, if we take both objectives seriously, our concern for peace should not be of the kind that makes men indifferent to real, fateful ideological and political choices; and our concern to prevent the spread of Communism should not be of the reckless kind which readily risks general war.

The role of Christians in various countries must certainly differ in the context of these two objectives. American Christians and Christians in Japan or India do not have exactly the same responsibility. The former may well be asked to remind themselves and their fellow citizens that the present world conflict is on its deepest level a conflict of ideas and convictions about the nature of society, rather than of military forces, and to keep to the fore understanding of the probable consequences of a nuclear war. The latter may well be asked to avoid the kind of refusal to take sides which involves moral and political indifference; and to recognize that the existence of military power in the non-Communist world, if it can only be wedded to a policy of restraint, may be necessary to preserve freedom of action for all the nations in that world. It is unlikely that those whose responsibilities and experiences profoundly differ will reach identical views on policy; but it may be possible for each to hold his opinion with a different spirit and emphasis if he becomes aware of the responsibilities and experiences of others. Christians in these contrasting situations should be able to engage one another in order to create this degree of mutual understanding. The reality of such engagement depends upon the frankest recognition of the way in which the differences of conviction are brought about by differences of experience.

3. *The Christian Citizen's Ultimate Decision.* The many factors so far mentioned which may help a Christian to form a judgment may still leave him somewhat in the air. It is essential to take one more step, which involves greater risk than any of the steps suggested earlier. It is essential to make choices between particular political parties or movements, between particular candidates, between particular legislative proposals, between particular policies and programs. The more concrete the commitment, the more difficult it is for the Christian citizen to be satisfied with it. It is difficult to say anything about this level of Christian decision which would have more than national or regional relevance. There is a difference between what is possible in a nation which has well-established democratic institutions with rather stable political parties, and what is possible in a new nation which is only now beginning to develop such institutions. The Christian who lives under a

regime that allows very little opportunity for participation by the citizen in the formation of public policy is in a still different situation. There are only two general statements which I shall make about this aspect of the Christian's decision as citizen.

The first is that the Christian cannot avoid being faced by it. There may be extreme cases in which the Christian should decide to oppose all of the existing political alternatives, and to wait for a new situation where new alternatives may be possible. But this is itself a decision; and while it may seem pure and safe, it may involve a measure of real irresponsibility, a premature renunciation of an opportunity to influence the situation positively. However, if such a choice is made, it does involve an obligation to do what can be done on a nonpolitical level to prepare the way for a situation in which the new alternatives may become available. There are few situations so hopeless that, even within the life of the church itself, nothing can be done to nourish a vision of better possibilities, or to preserve this vision for the following generation.

A second general statement is that, at this point of concrete political action, it is seldom desirable to organize a Christian political party or political movement. Christians in most cases should work in mixed parties and movements with non-Christians. Christian political movements create great confusion concerning the meaning of the gospel and the purpose of the church. There is real value in an organized Christian fellowship within a political movement, or a Christian voluntary group committed to one side of an issue which is controversial even among Christians; but care should be taken to avoid the suggestion that this represents the only Christian political way.

The Amsterdam Assembly's report (1948) on "The Church and the Social Disorder" expresses very well the reasons for the kind of caution that I am suggesting here.

It says of Christian political parties: "In general, the formation of such parties is hazardous because they easily confuse Christianity with the inherent compromises of politics. They may cut Christians off from the other parties which need the leaven of Christianity, and they may consolidate all who do not share the political principles of the Christian party not only against that party but against Christianity itself." The report did go on to say, in the light of a situation which existed in Germany in 1948, that "it may be desirable in some situations for Christians to organize themselves into a political party for specific objectives, so long as they do not claim that it is the only possible expression of Christian loyalty in that situation." It would be well to add also that the Christian party should be allowed to die before it is hardened by time or corrupted by power.

The basis on which Christians and non-Christians should co-operate for social objectives will differ from country to country. In a country with a strong Christian tradition in its culture, the co-operation can often proceed on common moral assumptions which have, in large measure, a common origin in the direct or indirect influence of Christ. In countries with a quite different history it is necessary to take advantage of that common concern for justice, political freedom, and honest government which fortunately does exist both inside and outside the church in many situations. Christians may believe that the whole emphasis upon the importance of developments in history, upon the dignity and freedom of the person, has primarily a Christian origin. But let them not quarrel with others about this. Instead, let them thank God for every sign of such concern, no matter how those who share it may explain its source in their own hearts.

45

chapter **3**

The Christian and Political Authority

THE DOMINANT ATTITUDE in the New Testament to the political order is acceptance of it as the work of divine providence. Revelation 13 is the great exception,[1] and its presence in the New Testament is a good corrective for those whose attitude toward political authority is based solely on Romans 13. Romans 13 and First Peter 2 are the chief references for the favorable attitude toward the political order to which I have referred. They are, however, supported conditionally by the words of Jesus: "Render to Caesar the things that are Caesar's, and to God the things that are God's" (Mark 12:17). Those words could

---

[1] That is, if we accept the identification of "the beast" in Revelation 13 with the Roman Empire. In *The State in the New Testament,* Professor Oscar Cullmann emphasizes the point that the difference between Romans 13 and Revelation 13 is to be understood entirely in the light of the Roman state's demand for emperor worship which underlies the latter passage and which is an example of the state's stepping beyond the area within which it has a right to claim obedience.

46

also be used to reject the claims that Caesar makes when he usurps the place of God, and so they can be quoted also in support of Revelation 13.

In my first chapter I said that the New Testament is essentially a nonpolitical book and gave some of the reasons for this. The passages to which I have referred do not show great interest in the political order. That order is to be accepted as part of the world that will soon pass away; but there is no thought of the Christian taking any active political responsibility. One reason for this view, of course, is that Christians were then a small minority, without the possibility of influencing political institutions or political decisions in the Roman Empire. In Revelation 13, where Christians are enjoined to reject the empire and its rulers, there is no thought of active political resistance. All that was imagined and all that was possible was passive spiritual resistance, faithful endurance under persecution.

It is significant, in view of all the circumstances, that we have in the New Testament such strong statements in support of the "governing authorities." Paul shows a remarkable optimism about the state when he says: "For rulers are not a terror to good conduct, but to bad. Would you have no fear of him who is in authority? Then do what is good, and you will receive his approval, for he is God's servant for your good." He adds: "Therefore one must be subject, not only to avoid God's wrath but also for the sake of conscience" (Romans 13:3–5). Those words were written before there was any organized persecution of Christians by the Roman authorities. But it was during a period of such persecution that the author of First Peter says much the same thing: "Be subject for the Lord's sake to every human institution, whether it be to the emperor as supreme, or to governors as sent by him to punish those who do wrong and to praise those who do right" (1 Pet. 2:13–14). The sentence which follows suggests that there

47

is an element of prudent policy in this injunction: "For it is God's will that by doing right you should put to silence the ignorance of foolish men" (1 Pet. 2:15). It may be that the author was endeavoring to make sure that Christians, if they are to be persecuted, should not give any excuse for persecution apart from their steadfastness as Christians. They should not give any ground for the authorities to charge them with being lawless or politically rebellious. Professor John Knox suggests that "the author of First Peter is convinced that, once magistrates generally recognize that the only crime of Christians is that of being Christians, the persecutions will cease."[2]

Two Necessary Warnings

The New Testament and the great traditions of the church have given strong support to two warnings which are relevant to political life in every age. The first warning is against anarchism; that is to say, against the kind of political irresponsibility that is indifferent to the problem of order in society; and equally against the kind of optimism that assumes that in some future society it will be possible for order to be maintained without any coercive power residing in the state. This caution has been carried so far that it was long difficult for Christians of all the various traditions to recognize the right of political revolution; though in nearly all traditions, events have forced even the most reluctant Christians to recognize and even to make use of this right. But quite apart from the problem of revolution, the rejection of anarchy or of a stateless society as a goal has been almost universal in the Christian Church. The clearest reason for this is that Christian realism about the sinfulness of man on all levels of historical development emphasizes the need of the coercive state as a

---

[2] *Journal of Biblical Literature,* Vol. 72, Part 3, 1953.

protection against the obvious forms of crime, and against all the less criminal ways in which individuals and groups seek to take advantage of one another. One of the most important differences between Christianity and Communism is at this point; for Communism in its theory looks for a time in history when there will be no need for a state with the authority to coerce.

The other warning which is clear in all the New Testament passages to which I have referred, but which is dramatized in the Book of Revelation, is the warning against the absolute state, the state that puts itself in the place of God. Paul emphasizes the limits of the state when he says that "there is no authority except from God." And yet, when Paul's words in Romans 13 are taken in isolation as the foundation for a Christian political philosophy, they are easily misused by those who see in them a divine sanction for every existing order rather than an affirmation that the authority of the state is always subordinate to the overriding authority of God. Words in Acts 5:29: "We must obey God rather than men," and the Book of Revelation, have fortunately helped to deliver Christians from a one-sided interpretation of Romans 13. This is one very clear example of the way in which arguing from the words of one text in Scripture, without considering the message of Scripture as a whole, can do great harm. It is often necessary to appeal from a particular passage to the Christian revelation as a whole, and in this case to the judgment of God over all things human, including nations and rulers.

The warning against anarchy has often been understood in the sense that the most that Christians should ever do by way of resistance to even the most tyrannical and lawless state is to refuse to obey, and to take the consequences in the form of punishment and persecution. Even Luther and Calvin, who were not passive by nature, had great difficulty in suggesting anything more than passive resistance to the most tyrannical political authorities. Both, however, in different contexts did provide for active political resistance on the part of lower political authorities against higher authorities. This loophole for active resistance, even for violent revolution, became a major factor in the history of Calvinism; and as a result, Calvinism helped to inspire revolutions in many countries, including Scotland, England, Holland, and the United States. In the period of the National Socialist state, many Lutherans approved of active political resistance in Norway, Denmark, and Germany. Roman Catholics have in general had less difficulty than Protestants in approving active political resistance, in situations where the political authorities have threatened the life or freedom of the church.

There are few more fascinating stories in Christian history than the story of the development of the attitude of Christians toward political revolution. They began with a powerful theological prejudice against it, supported by New Testament texts; but today there is no widely influential segment of the church which would refuse, on religious grounds, to admit that there are any circumstances in which political revolution is justified. In some circles there would be strong pacifist objection to violent revolution, but that is on a quite different level from the traditional theological condemnation of every form of political resistance.

The Christian warning against anarchy is in all circumstances a valid warning against an easy acceptance of revolution. To incite people to political revolt, before all orderly means of correcting an intolerable situation have been tried, or to do so without seeing near at hand the possibility of establishing a new and better order, would be irresponsible. Passive resistance, or even active efforts to frustrate the designs of an unjust, persecuting, and tyrannical state, may sometimes be justifiable, even when there is no possibility of a new order in sight. Political disobedience of this kind may be necessary in particular cases to help persecuted persons to escape from the arm of the persecuting state. But participation in such limited efforts is quite different from engaging in an organized revolt. The latter remains a possibility under rare circumstances; but the risk of long-continued anarchy, which may result in an even worse tyranny, should always be in the minds of Christians.

Responsibility and Participation

As we read the New Testament on "the governing authorities" (Romans 13) and the "emperor" and "governors" (1 Pet. 2:13), and as we reflect on what these words have often meant in Christian history, it is important to realize that the situation which they presuppose is very different from that which exists when the authorities are in some degree responsible to the people. In the next chapter I shall discuss the attitude of Christians to political democracy; here it is enough to state the fact that in many countries either the institutions which now exist, or those to the development of which most people are committed, are institutions of popular government. Wherever these are present, even though they may be highly defective, the idea of the authorities as *over against* the people ceases to be relevant. We cannot regard such authorities as having been providentially appointed by God to be *over against* the people; but we may regard the channels by which the people appoint them as being themselves providential.

Those who represent the authority and power of the state, even under systems of popular government, do at times seem to stand over against the people, or at least against some of the people. This is true most obviously of those who are caught by the law as criminals. And yet it is significant that under many systems of law even criminals are tried by juries made up of people of the same status as themselves. This is a symbol of the fact that even the state which judges them is not very distant from them. When the state exercises its right to conscript its citizens for purposes of national defense, the individual who is conscripted and his family may for the moment feel that the state is over against them; but in many cases they themselves may in principle believe that the system of conscription is fairer than other methods of dealing with the problem of national defense. In the United States the actual decisions about drafting individuals for national service are made by boards consisting of their neighbors, whose own sons are also liable to be drafted.

In countries which retain the principle of monarchy, it may be that the state, represented in the person of the ruler, is still in some sense "over against the people"; and yet in many cases it would be more accurate to say that the monarch is a symbol of the unity of the people, who in fact control the state. The monarch may also symbolize the continuity of the people with their own past. He may symbolize many historically given elements in the state; but often these historically given elements themselves involve the constantly growing power of the people over the state.

Today in many countries the Pauline doctrine of obedience to the governing authorities needs to be translated not only into current language, but also in terms of new concepts concerning the relationship between the state and the people. I suggest that the words "responsibility" and "participation" are more adequate in expressing this relationship than the word "obedience." At some points the citizen must obey the law because it is the law; but even in those cases he does so because he feels personally responsible for the sanctity of law, and for the maintenance of orderly processes in his community. If occasions arise when he believes that he must disobey the law for the sake of conscience, he does so with great reluctance because he has this sense of responsibility, and he should attempt to counteract any unintended consequences of his own defiance of the law. His responsibility includes also responsibility to do what he can to change the law when it is unjust. His responsibility includes the obligation to participate in the everyday processes by which the "authorities" are chosen and by which laws are made or repealed. Here I am speaking only of those countries where citizens do have the opportunity to participate in this way. Obedience to God in those situations is not the same as mere submission to those who are immediately in authority. It involves responsibility to keep those in authority under criticism, to help them to fulfill their functions better than it may be their intention to do, and to prepare to displace them by orderly processes when this seems to be in the interests of better government. Always it involves the responsibility to surround those in authority with laws which are themselves under a continuous judgment, and in the formation of this judgment Christian citizens should play their part.

chapter **4**

The Christian and Political Structures

ARE THERE ANY FORMS of political structure which Christian citizens everywhere should seek to establish or preserve? In recent years there has been a great concern on the part of representative Christians to avoid the identification of Christianity and the church with particular economic systems such as capitalism or socialism. The Christian faith transcends the institutions and the ways of life of particular cultures. It is therefore necessary to approach this question of the relationship of Christianity with political structures of any kind with great reserve. Certainly we cannot say that the particular form of government which we associate with any one country should be accepted as the best for all the other countries in the world. And yet I believe that some things have been learned about political life which make it possible that Christians should recognize a kinship between their faith and a certain kind of political structure, such as does not exist between that faith and other types of structure.

In so far as it is possible to do so, Christians should work to establish, to preserve, or to improve political structures which have the following two elements: (1) government that is based upon the consent and the participation of the people; and (2) constitutional protections for the rights of minorities to organize politically and to express their convictions.

These are the two most important aspects of political democracy. These aspects of democracy have developed in particular nations; but it is not for that reason impossible that they should represent some principles which have been so clearly established by experience as valid that they should be made available in one form or another as widely as possible. I write this as an American who has come to take the values in such democratic institutions for granted; and I realize that what I say may at first seem to be no more than praise for familiar aspects of my own culture. Yet, while there are real difficulties at this point, I believe that preference for these elements in democracy is now so general that we need not think of them as merely Western products. Most of the new nations which have been established in Asia have embodied these elements of democracy in their own constitutions.

It is significant that Karl Barth, who, more than any other theologian, has warned us to avoid the identification of Christianity and the church with the assumptions and institutions of particular cultures, has emphasized the kinship between Christianity and what he calls "the intentions of democracy." That is a good way to put it, because it is so easy to point to the failure to fulfill these intentions in some of the actual practices of democratic nations. Barth writes as follows:

> It must be admitted that the word and the concept "democracy" ("rule of the people") is powerless to describe even approximately the kind of State which, in

the Christian view, most nearly corresponds to the divine ordinance. This is no reason, however, why it should be overlooked or denied that Christian choices and purposes in politics tend on the whole towards the form of State which, if it is not actually realized in the so-called "democracies," is at any rate more or less honestly intended and desired.[1]

He emphasizes especially the second of the two elements suggested above, constitutional protection for minorities. He says:

> The Church always stands for the constitutional State, for the maximum validity and application of the twofold rule (no exception from and full protection by the law), and therefore it will be against the degeneration of the constitutional State into tyranny or anarchy.[2]

The Responsible Society

These two elements of political structure to which I refer are embedded in the concept of "the Responsible Society," which has been used by both the Amsterdam (1948) and the Evanston (1954) Assemblies of the World Council of Churches to indicate the political and economic goals to which Christians should be committed. The variety of senses in which the word "democracy" is used has prevented its general adoption in the ecumenical documents, and in this chapter I have no desire to emphasize the word. The Responsible Society as an ecumenical concept emphasizes three directions of responsibility—the responsibility of the community as a whole to God, the responsibility of the citizen for justice and public order in the community, and the responsibility of those who exercise power to the people whose lives are affected by it. The Amsterdam report (Section 3) said of the political aspect of the Responsible Society: "for a society to be responsible under

---

[1] *Against the Stream,* p. 44.
[2] *Ibid.,* p. 35.

modern conditions it is required that the people have freedom to control, to criticize and to change their governments, that power be made responsible by law and tradition, and be distributed as widely as possible through the whole community."

There was a great deal of ecumenical discussion of this concept of "the responsible society" between Amsterdam and Evanston, and we seem to have here a real development of social doctrine in the churches which has very wide support. Evanston fully confirmed what Amsterdam had said on this subject. Its report (the third section) emphasized the following four essential characteristics of the political institutions of the Responsible Society:

1. Every person should be protected against arbitrary arrest or other interference with elementary human rights.
2. Every person should have the right to express his religious, moral, and political convictions. This is especially important for those who belong to minorities.
3. Channels of political action must be developed by which the people can without recourse to violence change their governments.
4. Forms of association within society which have their own foundations and principles should be respected, and not controlled in their inner life by the state. Churches, families, and universities are dissimilar examples of this non-political type of association.

This concept of "the responsible society" does not directly define the pattern to which political institutions should conform, but it does suggest criteria by which all such institutions should be tested.

Participation in Responsibility

Now I shall return to the two elements of political structure which have already been emphasized—government based upon the consent and participation of the people, and freedom for minorities. The only form of democracy that is worth defending from a Christian point of view must have both. There is a type of democracy which is associated only with the rule of the majority, but this quickly becomes perverted if there are no effective protections for minorities. A nation may easily, without these protections, vote itself into tyranny. A popular political movement can sweep itself into power, and then so establish its power that it cannot be replaced, even after it has long since ceased to represent the will of the majority. No merely formal constitutional checks can prevent the majority from trampling on the rights of minorities, unless there are many within the majority who really believe in those rights, and who recognize that all citizens have a stake in their preservation.

When I say that government should be based upon the consent and the participation of the people, I refer to all the people. It may be that there should be some tests of competence which individuals must pass before they have the right to vote; but such tests should not be designed to exclude permanently any racial or economic group in the population. I do not suggest that every nation should move immediately to universal suffrage, though some of the great new nations have in recent years dared to do that. My only claim is that any society which prevents any one group from voting may be expected in the long run to exploit that group in the interests of other groups.

One of the most shocking denials of the true intentions of democracy in American life has been the denial of the vote to the Negro minority in some of the states. This situation has been greatly improved in recent years; but it was evident that where the Negro had no effective political rights, he was regularly the victim of discrimination in other spheres, even before the law. The final argument for the widest possible extension of voting rights is that those who are most likely to be denied it because they lack economic and social power are the very people whose needs are most easily neglected and who most easily become victims of injustice. They alone know how the institutions and the policies of the nation affect their lives. If they cannot speak for themselves, it is doubtful if anyone else can speak effectively on their behalf. Christians should be the first to recognize this, because they are aware of their own tendency to prefer their own interests and to neglect the interests of those whose lives are separated from their own.

Today, if it is possible to make a choice, the emphasis on constitutional protections for minorities is more urgent than the immediate extension of the suffrage. Once these protections are lost, the tendency today is to move toward a totalitarian society, in which those who hold the political power attempt to refashion the whole culture according to an ideological pattern, and in so doing destroy the spiritual freedom of persons. In this situation, truth ceases to be independent and is identified with the will of the powerful. The loss of freedom for minorities means that no independent voice can be raised on behalf of justice, and in the end, whatever the original intentions of those who control the state, justice comes to be as much the victim of this process as freedom. No one can say that in every case the process will lead to these results; but certainly they are a genuine threat whenever a society destroys the rule of law that protects minorities.

Biblical Factors in True Democracy

So far I have discussed the claims of a type of political structure that is characterized by popular government and by constitutional protections for minorities. I have said that there is an affinity between Christian faith and this type of political structure. And yet the facts of Christian history do

59

not altogether support this view. The classical periods of Christian thought and the period of the church's dominance in Europe do not suggest either that Christianity necessarily issues in popular government or that the church can be counted on to support freedom for minorities. The trend in most branches of the church has been in favor of constitutional aristocracy. The absolute state and all forms of lawless tyranny have generally been rejected. The Europe of the Middle Ages took it for granted that there was a divine law, with which the church and political rulers would equally be acquainted. But the idea of channels of consent and of participation by the people as an essential part of government did not gain wide acceptance until the modern period. Even the constitutionally safeguarded freedoms that did exist during the earlier history of the church did not include religious liberty for minorities. Neither Roman Catholics nor the majority of Protestants believed in religious liberty until after many struggles in the sixteenth and seventeenth centuries. It cannot be said that Christianity as such has until recently directly encouraged the rise of democratic political institutions. The most that can be claimed is that some of the Free Churches of Protestantism have since the seventeenth century made direct contributions to the development of democracy, and that there have been in the gospel from the beginning resources for democratic life which have been released by changes that have come in the modern period.

When I speak of these resources in the gospel for democratic life, I refer to three things especially. No one of these by itself need favor democratic institutions, but taken together they do. They are as follows:

1. The belief in the sovereignty of God over all the authorities and powers of the world is the ultimate guarantee, whether recognized or not, of the right and the duty of the person to claim for himself and for

60

his neighbors those kinds of freedom which a democratic constitution protects.

2. The recognition of and response to God's love for all persons, regardless of their status in society, is the ultimate basis, whether recognized or not, of the concern felt by men to raise up the poor and the defenseless and the disadvantaged to a position where they can develop their human capacities and maintain their just rights.

3. The Christian understanding of the pervasiveness of sin on all levels is the ultimate basis, whether recognized or not, of the political convictions which deny to any person or group arbitrary, unchecked power over others.

Any one of these essential elements in Christian faith can by itself be used for undemocratic purposes. The first has often been so used, when a particular group has claimed to have exclusive knowledge of the will of the sovereign God. The second easily loses its force when the third is not present, because it may seem to call for no more than acts of charity toward the poor, of a kind which in no way disturbs the existing distribution of power in society. The third, in isolation from the others, can be used to support a social pessimism which lays emphasis only on order, and on the danger of anarchy prevailing if the existing state of affairs is disturbed.

Perhaps the most important change that came about in the thinking and behavior of Christians was their acceptance of the right of people to differ in religious conviction and to express their differences. So long as Christians believed themselves justified in enforcing religious uniformity upon a nation by using the police power of the state, there could be no effective freedom for minorities in any sphere. The story of the change in Christian thinking and attitudes on this subject is of immense interest. Christians learned some things because they were forced upon them by events, and then discovered that what they had newly learned was more in harmony with their essential faith than what they had previously held. I doubt if there is a clearer example of this than the cause of religious liberty.

Today Protestants everywhere have come to accept on principle the right of minorities to differ from them on matters of religion. They have come to see, what only a few pioneers among them saw in the seventeenth century, that religious faith cannot be coerced, and that to use the power of the state to force outward conformity, to intimidate or to bribe people to profess by word or deed what they do not believe, is to tempt them to hypocrisy, and so to sin against them.

Roman Catholics are still under the burden of a doctrine concerning "error" which can be used to justify discrimination by a Roman Catholic state against religious minorities. On the other hand, the Roman Catholic Church itself is deeply divided on this subject; and many of the ablest Roman Catholic thinkers today agree with Father John Courtney Murray, S.J., the leading American Roman Catholic exponent of this view, that "political experience has taught men that the worst way to cope with dissidence is by legal suppression of it." He adds: "Experience too has, I think, taught the Church that any attempt to establish or maintain religious unity by governmental coercion of dissenters does more harm than good to the Church." [3] The division in the Roman Catholic Church is not only between individual thinkers but, in this regard, the spirit of Catholicism in one nation differs profoundly from that in another. Where the Christian churches have come to accept the rights of religious minorities, including those of atheists, the way is clear for a full and deeply felt recognition of the need of all persons for spiritual and cultural freedom.

---

[3] "Governmental Repression of Heresy," reprinted from the *Proceedings of the Catholic Theological Society of America*, pp. 64–65.

Difficulties to Be Faced

So far in this chapter I have discussed the problem of political structure, without considering the extent to which what is possible in terms of political behavior depends upon the social and cultural situation. It is necessary to consider the development of the kind of political institutions which have been emphasized in relation to the actual alternatives which any nation faces. In what follows I shall describe some of the difficulties that stand in the way of the development of the kind of political institutions which may seem in general desirable.

THE TOTALITARIAN SITUATION [4]

The most difficult situation of all is to be under a totalitarian regime which is in principle hostile to the churches, though it may tolerate them to some degree and allow them a strictly limited area within which to function. What toleration there is depends upon the complete avoidance of any political activity by Christians, unless that activity is wholly in accord with the purposes of the state. In those situations, the chief temptation may be to allow oneself to be used by the state to give strength to its propaganda. It is useless for me in my situation to give advice to fellow Christians who must decide on a day-by-day basis how far they can co-

---

[4] The illustrations of totalitarianism are taken from Communist countries. It happens that today this form of totalitarianism is the most efficient, and the form that meets us most frequently as a unified threat on a world scale. We must never forget that there is a totalitarianism of the "right" which only recently was a nightmare in Europe, that there is in some countries a clerical form of totalitarianism, that there are groups in the democratic countries, not least in the United States, which have used totalitarian methods in their efforts to destroy Communist influence and even to counteract all influences to the left of center. When the worst has been said about the totalitarianism of the right, it is at present less monolithic, less effective, and less tempting to great masses of people than Communism.

operate with a state whose ideology and most of whose purposes they must reject. Actually, the most unjust state performs certain technical functions without which life cannot go on, and some co-operation with it is inevitable except for those who have gone underground or who are in prison. The Christian citizen under these conditions often finds that he can do two things. In the first place he can say No at the right times. He can refuse to give Christian sanction to the state's propaganda. He can refuse, often at great personal risk, to be used by the police or the courts in building up a case against others who are being persecuted. In the second place, he can in many face-to-face relations between persons bear a Christian witness, or it may be a witness to the claims of ordinary justice for a Christian reason.

I have been helped in understanding the kind of situation which I am describing by the writings of Charles C. West, based upon his studies of Christian life in eastern Germany. He has translated the following passages from a letter from a pastor in East Germany:

> Then we experienced that here and there a few of us began to talk to half and full Marxists with love. With love—that means undiplomatically, in all frankness and freedom, yet not self-righteously or moralistically. And almost everywhere where that happened, we saw that the evil spirits stole away and the sea became still. In the place of their dialectically grounded desire to liquidate us (for the moment largely rhetoric) came human respect and the assurance that they wouldn't do us any harm, because we were really "good honest people" whom one protects and defends. Then, here and there, something quite different occurred. Suddenly the mask, which looks so deceivingly like the real face, fell, and revealed a helpless man who sinks under his load of sin and guilt, and who clings to the Christian who has treated him with a bit of love, who hasn't lied to him like the others. . . .

A [Christian] factory research assistant was the only one who discussed with reason and facts in the compulsory Marxist weekly training courses for assistants. The other seventy kept still or made fun of it. In private they said to him: "Why do you expose yourself? You can't get anywhere in any case." One day he was suspended. Why was he so careless? The case was heard before the local union officials. With some anxiety he defended his position. Result: a few days later he was reinstated. To be sure—for how long? But all seventy greeted him respectfully and warmly. Often this is how people begin a little to praise their Father in Heaven, because they see good works which point to Him. And out of this, as a by-product, comes a bit more room for honest work in a profession. In this case also some room was gained for free science and scholarship, if only more people would move with conviction into this room.

This may seem too optimistic at some points, since East Germany is favored by having among its people very few believers in the state's ideology, and because what happens in East Germany cannot be kept from the knowledge of people in West Germany and in the outside world generally. But Mr. West's emphasis on the Christian's attitude and act in direct personal face-to-face relations does open up a whole world of possibilities of action for Christian citizens under what may seem to be the most unfavorable conditions.

Cannot Christians in these situations take one more step? Cannot they do much to preserve for their children through the church a vision of a society in which institutions are more favorable to justice and freedom? I do not mean that they should suggest that the road to that society is an easy one, or that, if it is reached, the result would bring a perfect solution of their problems. All that I want to stress here is that even under those circumstances, in which nothing can be done now about a better structure, Christians should not forget their responsibility to do what they can to make possible the coming into being of such a structure, should circumstances change. They should not in the life of their churches allow a tradition to become frozen which makes a virtue of ignoring all problems of political structure, and perhaps develops a theological defense of this attitude.

LACK OF SPIRITUAL BASIS IN NATIONAL LIFE

A second difficulty is the absence, from the culture of a particular nation, of the influences which in other nations have prepared the way for political institutions of the type here commended. Political institutions are never self-sufficient. The most perfect constitutional arrangements cannot be made to work unless in the nonpolitical life of the nation there are attitudes and habits which are favorable to them. Popular government and freedom for minorities are not likely to work unless among the people there is a considerable measure of mutual tolerance as between major social groups. This depends upon a very wide area of agreement about central social objectives. Unless there is a widespread concern for justice for the persons who have least power and privilege, political measures in their behalf are likely to be frustrated. If economic institutions provide no protections against landlords, creditors, or employers, and if the economic power in the nation is concentrated in the hands of a few, the real situation of people is likely to be determined by those economic realities, and not by the external form of political institutions.

There must be willingness to accept the results of an election, and patience with the orderly processes by which changes are effected. There must be many public servants who are honest and loyal to their responsibilities. Inevitably there will be a great deal of pushing and pulling as between various interests in any community; but unless the people involved have some sense of a public interest that transcends their own, the best political institutions are likely to be ineffective. Participation by the people in political life does depend upon habits of participation in other spheres. A pattern of authority in home and church and school which teaches people only to obey is not favorable to a democratic pattern in political life. Also, if there are few among the people who have a sense of obligation to truth or to standards that transcend the immediate will of those who hold power, there is not likely to be much incentive to establish or to preserve such institutions as protect the freedom of minorities. In the development of such institutions in Europe, the fact that there were religious minorities which struggled for the right to witness and to worship was often decisive in opening the door to freedom for all citizens.

The effect of my suggesting these various conditions in the life of a people, on which the working of desired political institutions depends, may be that many readers will say that they are impossible of fulfillment, and therefore that what I have written is irrelevant to their situation. These conditions are never perfectly fulfilled anywhere, and it is not possible to say in advance what degree of fulfillment is necessary if the kind of institutions which have been discussed in this chapter are to be reasonably effective. The mention of these conditions may help to indicate the breadth of the Christian citizen's responsibility. This responsibility is not in the first instance political; for the Christian must be concerned about those conditions which are deeper and more pervasive than political institutions and political decisions.

Authoritarian Traditionalism

Some readers of this book may live in countries in which the political institutions are not totalitarian, but are not moving toward democracy. It may be that the structure of these countries is somewhat traditional and authoritarian, but that their rulers do not have the totalitarian desire to control the whole life of the people, and fortunately lack the energy through which totalitarian states have been created. In such countries the churches may have a very large measure of freedom, and Christians as citizens may be able to do much in dealing with concrete problems of justice and welfare. Regimes of this sort are likely to experience great difficulty in dealing with large problems of technology and industry. They are likely to be financially corrupt. They will always have difficulty in standing up against pressures from outside.

Situations differ so much in detail from country to country that it is unprofitable to generalize concerning the responsibility of Christian citizens. But, in the context of this type of national situation, I do want to emphasize the conviction that Christians should not try to impose on their national life an abstract, ready-made pattern of political institutions, such as European or American democracy, which has been learned elsewhere. I do not mean that they should complacently accept the situation as it is, but that they should make that situation their starting-point, and make the most of the indigenous political habits and institutions; and that they should emphasize especially the cultural and economic changes on which more adequate political institutions would depend. There is often a great deal that can be done within the Christian Church, and moving from the church outward into the community, to help people to find new ways of living. But there is no book of rules for the Christian citizen in regard to such decisions; and he must be prepared at times to find that the old society needs drastic changes without delay, and that his best service is to associate himself with those who are organizing politically to make them possible.

Does Democracy Depend on Christianity?

How far are democratic political institutions dependent upon Christian influence in the surrounding culture? That is one of the most difficult questions which most readers of this book must ask. So far as the historical record goes, the nations which have been able to make democratic institutions work for a period of significant length have been countries with strong Christian influences in their culture. On the other hand, it is clear that some forms of Christianity have not proved favorable to the development of such institutions. That has tended to be true of Roman Catholicism where it has had a monopoly, and of Eastern Orthodoxy. One student of this subject, Professor James Hastings Nichols, goes so far as to say that the only forms of Christianity which have prepared the way for democracy have been those associated with what he calls Puritan Protestantism.[5] He includes under this term only the Calvinistic and the sectarian or "Free Church" forms of Protestantism. He would admit that Anglicanism has come to be a support for democratic life, and that Scandinavian Lutheranism constitutes a special problem. It is necessary to point out that one of the most highly disciplined and devout forms of Calvinism, that which we find in South Africa, is hardly democratic in its influence.

These historical considerations are helpful in some measure, but they are misleading if we project them uncritically on the future. The ecumenical experience of the past half century has resulted in much mutual influence of the churches one upon another. Whenever any branch of the church is in a minority, no matter how authoritarian its influence in other situations, it can mediate to the community aspects of the gospel which help to liberate people. This minority status, which frequently brings the best out

---

[5] See his *Democracy and the Churches,* Westminster Press, 1951.

of a religious tradition, is characteristic of many churches today. It enables churches to be more open to learning from each other. It makes them, whatever their theory, concerned about the problem of the spiritual freedom of all citizens from the power of the state.

The hardest question still remains: the possibilities in cultures which have felt only slightly the influence of Christ, where the Christian community constitutes so small a minority of the population that it is difficult to imagine that it can become a major factor, in any near future, in shaping a national culture. Here I can do no more than state a few propositions which I hope may form the basis for discussion.

1. The pressure of events on many nations has changed the alternatives available to them. The static authoritarian political institutions, to which I have referred in an earlier paragraph, may cease to be workable because of the development of a more modern technological society, or because of the example of neighboring countries which are experimenting with popular government, or which are under Communist control. Communism creates popular aspirations, even though its ultimate effect may be to frustrate them. Where there is considerable revolutionary ferment, there may be very little time for more gradual political changes; and the real alternatives available may be only a direct movement toward democratic institutions or one toward Communist totalitarianism. The fact that the alternatives are so limited may awaken a new vision and a new sense of responsibility among those who are able to lead the people. There is no guarantee that this will be the case, but there are countries where something like this is happening now.

2. It is largely a matter of speculation, but there is a possibility that the influences which were necessary for the original development of democratic institutions in the West

will not be needed in the same strength as new nations seek to establish those institutions. I am not suggesting that it will now be possible to transplant institutions from one country to another, but rather that new institutions may grow partly out of interaction with the experience of those who have a strong democratic tradition.

3. Christians must thank God for common convictions which they share with non-Christians, whether these be adherents of other religions or men without religious affiliation, who care for social justice and for the dignity of all persons, who show forth in many ways their belief in democratic institutions and their integrity as citizens. In particular cases, non-Christians have been ahead of Christians in the understanding of the needs of their country and in their commitment to the goals emphasized in this book. Even where this is true, it may often be fairly claimed that the direct or indirect influence of Christ can be seen in their vision of truth. But Christians would do well to avoid trying to establish the claim that democratic movement is always due to Christian influence, and to be open to the uncharted ways in which God brings pressure to bear upon his people.

4. The influence of a Christian community upon a nation in which it is a small minority can be far greater than its numerical strength suggests. The indirect influence of Christ is already present in many ways; but a Christian community whose members are alert can do more than they may imagine to strengthen the influences which are favorable to the freedom and dignity of persons, and to integrity and responsibility in public life.

PROBLEMS TOO URGENT FOR DEMOCRACY?

A final difficulty and, in the short run, the most urgent is that in some nations the problems which call for solution are so deep and pressing that many are tempted to conclude that the slow processes of democracy are inadequate. The attraction of the Communist short cut, which promises both a technological and a social revolution in a relatively short time, is always at hand to make people impatient with democratic methods. Geographical proximity to Communist countries may increase this attraction, and may make all too easy the penetration of a country by Communist agents. It also may at some point, because of the threat of Communist military power, create the tendency among those who waver at all to choose the side which will be safer in case the Communists win control. All these factors combine to make it easy for people to calculate that their country may not have time enough to make the necessary changes by orderly political process.

I shall deal in the next chapter with some of the problems raised specifically by Communism, but here I want to lay great emphasis on a single point: the kind of political institutions about which I have been writing do depend for their stability and their health upon economic institutions which are organized for the benefit of the people as a whole. Neither control of land by a small number of landlords nor control of industry by a small group of employers is in the end compatible with political democracy. The protection of the rights of the tiller in his use of land and the development of labor unions are indispensable. The prevention of industrial crises which cause large-scale unemployment must be a function of government as trustee for the whole national community. Where poverty is very great because of pressure of the population on the food supply, national planning is essential to increase production and to raise the standard of living. Great inequalities of wealth, which divide a nation into two worlds of rich and poor, are a cancer that it must be the purpose of every nation to overcome.

These things are very easy to write, but they raise problems which are often overwhelming. In many instances, a national economy is dependent for its health upon the policies of other countries, often on those of my own country. The raising of standards of living in the so-called "technically undeveloped countries" requires international planning and investments from abroad, accompanied by safeguards against enonomic imperialism. Americans will need to accept the fact that the type of free enterprise which they prefer may not have the same dominant place in the economies of countries that must move quickly to raise their standard of living. In many of these countries, the state will necessarily assume larger economic functions than in the United States (though its economic functions even there are far greater than is usually believed). People in all countries should recognize the danger that an economic system which is at all points controlled by the state may lack the vitality that comes from the encouragement of many centers of economic initiative, and will almost certainly concentrate both political and economic power in too few hands.

The Evanston Assembly of the World Council of Churches (1954), through the report of its third section on "Social Problems," should be a help to all of us in its emphasis that, if we think in terms of such fixed and theoretical concepts as "capitalism" and "socialism," we can reach no useful conclusion, and that what is needed is that we should move toward economies which in varying patterns combine state planning and regulation with freedom and flexibility.

No words can do justice to the need of social and economic revolution in many countries; it is most difficult for words written in New York to do so. More than half of the people in the world live on a level of bare subsistence economically, and lack the protections against disease and famine which are taken for granted in more privileged countries. The statistics concerning expectancy of life at birth, which range from as low a figure in some countries as thirty years to as high a figure in other countries as sixty-eight years, are most revealing concerning the real human consequences of differences in standards of living. Christian citizens in every country, especially those in the richer countries, must give first place to the responsibility to do what they can do to secure for these hundreds of millions of persons deliverance from such conditions of poverty and distress. The motive for much that is done may be in the minds of many the desire to check the growth of Communism, but for Christians this can never be more than a secondary motive. Primarily for them it should be a simple concern for justice prompted by love.

THE SIGNIFICANCE OF LOCAL COMMUNITY

I began this chapter by stressing the significance of political structures, but I have tried to make clear that political structures are not self-sufficient. They can be empty forms; they can fail to work at all, or they can be misused and perverted, unless there are influences among the people which encourage responsible living, and which are favorable to tolerance and to justice. One essential factor is the habits which come from the experiences of living in many small groups. There is a danger that we may put too much emphasis on world-shaking problems, and not enough on the development of community life in a village or in a parish. The Christian as citizen must begin with the most immediate local responsibilities. His opinions and his votes concerning large-scale political issues are important; but frequently, while he may be able to do very little about these issues, he can do a great deal about the local school, or the extension of health services, or the improvement of

74

farming methods, or about the spirit of the community in his immediate neighborhood. Often what he does in his own parish can have surprising indirect effects upon the life of the community. The Lucknow Study Conference (1952), to which I have referred, emphasized the role of the church in this context in these words: "The Church's aim should be to build up cells of true community-living as a means of humanizing the impersonal relationships of modern large societies."

chapter **5**

The Issues Raised by Communism

OFTEN IN THIS BOOK there have been references to the effect of Communism upon the life of all our nations. Some nations are under the control of Communist governments. I live in a nation which is known for the decisiveness of its anti-Communist policies, in relation both to any internal threat of Communist penetration and to the spread of international Communism in the world. There are other nations which are equally decisive in rejecting Communism for themselves, but which regard the policies of the United States with mixed feelings. They welcome the fact that there is a strong center of both military and economic power in the non-Communist world; but they fear that the United States is at times reckless, a prey to anti-Communist hysteria, and they do not want to be too dependent on American power. There are other nations which, whatever their official policies, are in some degree vulnerable to Communist penetration because they have desperate economic problems for which Communism promises quick and ready solutions. Partly because of their geographical situation they attempt to develop foreign policies which are at least noncommittal in the international conflict in which Russia and China and the United States play leading roles.

Christian citizens in these quite different situations are sure to see the world differently. Christians in America need to understand far better than they do why Christians in, for example, India or Japan do not emphasize the same objects of hope and fear as Christians in America. I believe that Christians in India or Japan need to give more emphasis than some of them do to the totalitarian aspect of Communism, and to the danger that international Communism may destroy the existing political independence of nations.

There is one difference which needs to be understood quite generally—the difference between Christians who live in countries where it is natural to associate daily with Communists as human beings, and those who hardly see a Communist from one year to the next, and think of Communism only in terms of distant political figures who have become evil symbols rather than persons. Mr. Adlai Stevenson noted this difference on a trip around the world in 1953. He reported: "Nor do all our friends who share our view about Communism, share our views about Communists. I recall the anti-Communist Catholic youth delegation that called on me in France and left a friend outside in the car because he was a Communist." [1]

The Nature of Social Revolution

Whatever we say about Communism, we should begin by recognizing that far deeper than Communism in many countries today is the fact of social revolution. This is in part a nationalistic revolution against foreign rule. It is in

---

[1] *Call to Greatness*, p. 31.

part a rising of colored peoples against the racial arrogance of white men, who have assumed a natural right to supremacy in the world. It is in part a revolt against inherited feudal structures and various forms of economic oppression. Always there is present the belief that such technological changes are possible as will deliver mankind from most of its present burden of poverty, hunger, and disease. At one of the most representative Christian conferences ever to meet in Asia, the Bangkok Conference of 1949, it was declared:

> In considering Communism, the Christian must distinguish between the social revolution which seeks justice and the totalitarian ideology which interprets and perverts it. The Christian Church must welcome the demand of the peoples for a fuller participation in the life of society at the level where power is exercised, since this is an expression of human dignity; and the rise of Communism is a judgment on the Churches for their failure to do so. Nevertheless the struggle for justice frustrates itself if the evil forces inherent in any human situation are not held in check. Because Communism lacks a conception of the independence of moral reality over against power, it denies the supremacy of the moral law over power-politics and hence in the long run defeats the very purpose of the social revolution. This ideological error in Communism, which turns a social revolution for justice into a new oppression, arises out of the self-righteousness of its militant atheism; and at this point the conflict between Christianity and Communism is fundamental.

When I speak of Communism in this book I refer to a particular political movement, which acknowledges the authority of Marx and Lenin, which has its base in the Soviet Union, and which is embodied in Communist parties around the world. This movement is not difficult to identify, and Communism in this quite definite sense should be distinguished from a much broader use of the word, which would include many Christian Communist experiments from the days of the New Testament to the present time. It may be unfortunate to surrender the word "Communism" to those who give it this definite political meaning, but it is doubtful if we can avoid doing so without causing great intellectual confusion.

Communism in this modern sense had its origin in the wholly justified revolt of both mind and conscience against the inhumanities of nineteenth-century capitalism in Western industrialized countries. The impulse from this early Marxism had much to do with the actual changes which took place in the older capitalistic societies, upsetting the Marxist predictions of future developments, and making those societies almost immune to the propaganda of contemporary Communism. However, while recognizing that this earlier Marxism was a very important stimulus in the development of working-class movements and of radical criticism of *laissez faire* capitalism among the intellectuals in Western countries, we must emphasize also the contribution of Christian social movements and the broader impact of democracy on Western industrial society. The changes in the Anglo-Saxon countries, which have resulted in far more democratic and humane economic institutions, did not come primarily from Marxist influence.

It was the remarkable achievement of Lenin to make Marxism into a strategy for revolution in countries which have not been greatly industrialized, and where capitalism has not been far advanced. He made Marxism relevant to the Russian situation and to the agricultural countries of Asia. He made it the promise of emancipation for all the peoples which regarded themselves as victims of Western imperialism. It is one of the ironies of modern history that Communism is strongest in the very countries which, because of their lack of developed capitalistic institutions, the early Marxists would not have regarded as ripe for revo-

79

lution; whereas the advanced capitalistic countries were able to democratize and humanize their economic institutions in time to make a Communist revolution superfluous.

Communism—as Judgment and as Tyranny

The first thing which Christians should say about this whole Communist development is that it represents a form of divine judgment upon the white race, and upon the nations and classes which have until recently run the world largely for their own benefit. It is a judgment on the churches. The Amsterdam report (the third section) did not exaggerate when it said that "it is one of the most fateful facts in modern history that often the working classes, including tenant farmers, came to believe that the churches were against them or indifferent to their plight." The atheism of Communism stems in part from the relations between science and religion in the mid-nineteenth century; but it also stems from the socially irrelevant or socially reactionary character of so much Christianity during the period in which the Marxist movement took shape.

The second thing which Christians should say about Communism is that this instrument of judgment upon the white, middle-class world has become the means by which a tyranny has become fastened upon many nations, which is more oppressive than the old political regimes or economic systems from which it had "liberated" them.

If we look for the reason for this tragic development, I think that we can find it in one primary fact about Communism: it is a total system of life and thought which is absolutely exclusive in its claims. Christianity is also exclusive at some points; but it does not claim to have answers to all questions in all spheres of life, and all its answers stand under the questioning of God who transcends all the authorities and powers in the world and in the church.

80

To put it another way: under the Communist regime, those who control power in the state are the only teachers with freedom to teach, and are the priests of a secular faith which is fanatically believed. The atheism of Communism deprives the Communist society of any judgment from without. The completeness and exclusiveness of the Communist scheme mean that in a Communist society there is a consolidation in one place of all of the centers of thought, inspiration, and power. The freedom of the mind and of the spirit of man depends upon preserving many centers of thought, inspiration, and power. The situation is made even worse by the international character of Communism, because of which there is in the Communist world no chance to win freedom by moving from one country to another.

There are two consequences of this total and exclusive Communist view of life which I want to emphasize. The first is that anyone who holds this view has a ready excuse for using any methods, however cruel, in advancing his cause. If you believe that you and your movement alone have the only and the final solution of the problems of human life, it is easy to convince yourself that any means by which you gain or preserve your power to impose that solution will be justified. If your particular philosophy, because of its materialism, has little place for the depths of the human person, and, because of its atheism, knows no God who loves even your opponents and your enemies, it is easy to deal with all persons who oppose you as mere things to be removed by the most efficient methods available.

The other consequence of the Communist view of life has to do with the future. The Communist believes sincerely that the only cause of evil in human life is to be found in the system of private property, whether this be capitalistic or feudal. He sincerely believes that there is no independent source of evil in the will-to-power that is expressed in

81

the state. He concludes that when the revolution has finally succeeded in destroying the roots of the old economic system, there will be no class divisions and that the state as a coercive agent will wither away. Notice the result: the Communist can put all his emphasis on finishing the task of revolution by any means that he believes necessary, being confident that his success in doing this will ensure not only justice but also freedom. He need not worry lest any permanent evil effects should follow upon concentration of power in the state or upon the state's ruthlessness, for all such effects will disappear when the coercive state withers away. This seems to me to be the greatest single miscalculation of Communism. It means that the Communist never has to plan for freedom. Freedom is expected to come as a by-product of successful revolution. The Christian understanding of life, based as it is on the belief that pride, selfishness, and the will-to-power appear on all levels of human development, and often become most destructive when they are least expected, represents a complete contrast to the Communist view of the future.

Communism—Temptation and Peril

In countries where Communism is a real temptation, because it seems to be the only political movement which deals drastically enough with current problems, and because it promises to the people of a country a new start, some Christians may become convinced that they should give a measure of support to the Communist party. This is the more likely to occur because it is the Communist tactic to emphasize chiefly national grievances in the party's appeal to those who are not members of it. The party's official position on religion is hardly mentioned or is explained away, as are the totalitarian aspects of the Communist-controlled state.

Communists will try to win the peasants by promising them private ownership of land—and yet it is their intention at a later stage to bring in collective ownership of it. The amazing success of the Communists in many situations in using immediate and acceptable goals to obscure their ultimate objectives creates great confusion even among Christians. The threat of international Communism to the effective political independence of nations under Communist control is extraordinarily well hidden, where Communism joins forces with nationalism and appeals strongly because of its promise of liberation from imperialism.

Christian citizens in some countries may be led to think that support for Communism may help to rid their country of much social injustice, but that the cultural totalitarianism of Communism can be counteracted by other forces in their national life. Or, at worst, they may believe that a Communist regime, oppressive as it would be, would pass away in a generation or so, and leave a deposit of social reform which could be brought about by no other method now in sight. I think that Christians who come to these conclusions have underrated the total claims of Communism, and have assumed that their country under Communism would have more freedom from domination from abroad, from Russia or, possibly, China, than is likely in view of past experience to be the case. Even political cooperation with the Communist party on the part of a non-Communist leftist party, or the formation of a coalition government, is likely to put the Communist party in complete control.

Christians sometimes think that they will be able to use the Communists for their own ends; but before they try to do this, it would be wise for them to look around to see if there are any cases in which such efforts did not result in the Christians being used by the Communists for Communist ends. Two Indian Christians, P. D. Devanandan and

83

M. M. Thomas, have written a helpful book entitled *Communism and the Social Revolution in India*. They go very far in sympathizing with those who feel the strong attraction of Communism; but they put the main difficulty in these words:

> Because it is an integral whole, Communism cannot be understood in parts. It may be that in its initial approach it isolates one or other of these aspects from the whole. But that is part of the Communist strategy, to use one or other of these emphases as the thin end of the wedge and eventually to push in the whole system, the total thing. Communism stands or falls as a totality, and as such it should be accepted or rejected.[2]

One of the lessons which have been learned in recent years is that some forms of anti-Communism are sterile or destructive. Christians should oppose the Communist ideology and propaganda, and they should do what they can politically to prevent the extension of Communist power; but mere negations here are not enough.

Christians who are not tempted by Communism need to understand why Communism makes a strong appeal in many situations to sensitive and thoughtful minds. Some of their fellow Christians believe that, mistaken as the ultimate Communist convictions about God and man and history are, the Communist explanation of their country's contemporary situation is convincing, and that the Communist program to meet their country's problems is the best or the least unsatisfactory available. One difficulty is the chasm between those who live under conditions which make almost any change seem desirable, and those who have much which they want to conserve and who fear that any radical change will be for the worse. My own countrymen are in the latter situation, whereas a large part of the human race is in the former.

---

[2] *Communism and the Social Revolution in India*, p. 17.

The appeal of Communism to students and intellectuals often comes from the fact that it provides them with a total philosophy of life which satisfies their minds, and an object of commitment which fills an empty place in their hearts. As Devanandan and Thomas say of modern intellectuals in India: "Religion has failed to provide a 'framework within which to organize their thoughts' about nature and man and history."[3] Communism provides such a framework. It is easy to criticize this from the vantage point of Christian faith; but, if a person has never been exposed to a relevant interpretation of Christian faith, it is not surprising that he finds Communism convincing.

It is a mistake to divorce the place which Communism fills as a substitute for religion, as an interpretation of life, and as an object of commitment, from its social program. The thing which makes it effective as a substitute for religion is that it seems to be relevant to the social problems of some nations. Many who accept Communism on this intellectual and spiritual level may not themselves belong to the poorest classes, but often they are concerned about the poverty and the misery around them, or see in Communism the promise of more effective government and of a better status in the world for the people of their country. Beyond the circle of those who become convinced Communists, the Communist party wins support because it appeals so skillfully to all the grievances which are felt by the people of an area.

I have emphasized the positive attraction of Communism in some countries, but this is only one aspect of the power of Communism in the world today. It need not attract more than a small minority. If it is able to gain control of government through politically skillful use of this minority or by revolution, it then coerces the majority.

---

[3] *Ibid.*, p. 7.

If there is a Communist army not far away, its very existence may frighten people into submission. We should see this whole picture; but Communism does not usually threaten a country unless there is a strategically placed minority, often strongest among intellectuals and among industrial workers, which is convinced of the truth of the claims of Communism, and unless the nation in general is vulnerable to penetration because of the weakness of government and because of long-neglected economic problems.

False Forms of Anti-Communism

There are two forms of anti-Communism against which Christian citizens everywhere should be on their guard. The first is the tendency to put major trust in military preparations. I believe that it is necessary for non-Communist countries to have military strength. If the only strong military forces were in the Communist world, the nations outside that world would easily become subject to military pressure. A balance of military power is no final guarantee of peace or freedom, but it does help us to gain time for more constructive efforts. Even people in nations which emphasize their neutrality may admit that if there were no such balance of military power, their own freedom of movement would be severely limited.

The other form of anti-Communism which is most destructive is the kind of panic which sacrifices civil liberties in order to prevent subversive activity. It is one of the ironies of the phenomenon known as McCarthyism in the United States that it has damaged, for a time at least, the very liberties which make democratic institutions worth defending against Communism; it has created dissension and confusion in America, and undermined in some measure the morale of the non-Communist world. As I write, it seems that this particular phenomenon is rapidly losing ground; but our experience with it remains a warning

86

against the dangers of a blind and hysterical form of anti-Communism.

The Evanston report (the third section) summarized well both the dilemma and the task of Christians in relation to Communism in these words:

> It will be the task of the Churches to point to the dangers inherent in the present situation: on the one hand the temptation to succumb to anti-Communist hysteria and the danger of self-righteous assurance concerning the political and social systems of the West; on the other hand the temptation to accept the false promises of Communism and to overlook its threat to any responsible society.

chapter 6

Christian Action—Peril and Hope

THE CHRISTIAN as a citizen will naturally be guided in part by the hope that what he decides to do or to support will have favorable results. We cannot separate motives from intended consequences, and we are irresponsible if we do not use our brains to calculate as well as we can what the actual consequences are likely to be. If there is no hope at all for any overt political action in a national situation, the Christian may have to wait and give his full attention to the things that can be done to prepare the way for future action, which is not now possible; or, perhaps, he should concern himself only with personal witness and with personal acts of helpfulness in the immediate situation. There are times when nonpolitical action within the Christian community itself can have great political consequences. That is true, for example, when the church by being true to itself preserves in society a voice that is independent of the state, and in doing so keeps the door open, if only a little, for political freedom.

Our hope for the results of our choices as citizens does in some degree influence the direction of our action. And yet, action usually involves risk. Our calculations of consequences may easily be mistaken. In an earlier chapter it was emphasized that many of the most fateful decisions which we are called upon to make today do involve this risk. To permit the risk to cause us to withdraw from action is no road to moral security, because inaction on our part often has an indirect effect which involves the same kind of risk. Christian citizens can neither ignore the hope for favorable results nor refuse to act until hope becomes assurance of success.

Action in obedience to the best light which we can find concerning God's will for us and for our society will not be absolutely secure action. It should be taken in faith that God will use what is good and true in the action, in its intentions as well as in its results, for the fulfillment of his purposes. It should be action accompanied by repentance for whatever in it is the expression of self-centeredness and pride. Such faith and such repentance should not be regarded as religious substitutes for thinking and doing as well as we can in practical and political concerns. Non-Christian citizens have every right to feel contempt whenever religion is used by Christians as a substitute for knowledge or effort. But faith and repentance, in the context of the understanding in Christ of God's overruling authority and of God's forgiveness, should increase energy and courage for action. It should make possible the difficult and essential combination of resoluteness with charity.

The total outlook for the future should not be insistence on the hope of endlessly cumulative progress, nor should it be a dogmatic pessimism which denies all hope for society in this world. We know that evil in our hearts is stubborn, and that it appears on all levels of cultural and political development; that the possibilities of the tyrannical use of power and of the destructiveness of war are by-products of the same advances in civilization which make possible the overcoming of poverty and the emergence of a world-wide community. History is not merely a platform on which individuals are prepared for inward blessings or for eternal life. Nor, as a record of man's collective life, is history a story of a vast and unified success. And yet within it there have been and there will be many communal and institutional embodiments of justice and fraternity, which have value to the Lord of history. They are all of them partial, and marked by man's sin as well as by true loyalty and love. If they pass away, they remain as possibilities to be realized again, and the record of them may inspire generations that know them only as a memory. To work for such communal and institutional embodiments of justice and fraternity is to serve the kingdom of God, even though that kingdom far transcends them and by it they are judged.

The Fellowship of the Church

The Christian citizen, as he tries to find his way, does not have to go alone. He is a member of a church which should help him in his citizenship. Churches may often fail in this, and at times the Christian may have to rebel against the outlook of the church in a particular time and place. He can appeal from that limited outlook to the witness of some segment of the larger church. Often the best appeal may be to the teaching that we find in the reports of the great conferences of the church at Oxford and Amsterdam and Evanston. But the church in a given country or in a particular parish should seek to help its members at the points of difficulty which have been so much emphasized in this book. It should mediate to its members the judgment of God from beyond their nation or their social group. It should bring together Christians who have common problems, so that they may learn from each other. It should encourage experts within the Christian community to contribute what guidance they have to give. It should help Christians who belong to different races and nations, whose experiences are in sharp contrast, who tend to be on opposite sides of public questions, to correct one another.

Always the church should be the teacher and inspirer of its members as they act in the world, and, when necessary, it should be for them a home, where in perplexity or under pressure from hostile forces they may find both light and healing.

List of the Great Ecumenical Conferences

1910: Edinburgh—World Missionary Conference
1925: Stockholm—Christian Conference on Life and Work
1927: Lausanne—World Conference on Faith and Order
1928: Jerusalem—International Missionary Council
1937: Oxford—Conference on Church, Community, and State
1937: Edinburgh—World Conference on Faith and Order
1938: Madras-Tambaram—International Missionary Council
1947: Whitby, Ontario—International Missionary Council
1948: Amsterdam—First Assembly of the World Council of Churches
1952: Lund—World Conference on Faith and Order
1952: Willingen—International Missionary Council
1954: Evanston, U.S.A.—Second Assembly of the World Council of Churches